Vantage Press, Inc.

516 West 34th Street
New York, N. Y. 10001

Me: The New American Teenager

*A Poem, Accompanied by
Other Poetic Creations*

Randolph Nelson Levy

*Randolph Nelson Levy
October 1993*

VANTAGE PRESS
New York

FIRST EDITION

Copyright © 1993 by Randolph Nelson Levy

Published by Vantage Press, Inc.
516 West 34th Street, New York, New York 10001

Manufactured in the United States of America
ISBN: 0-533-10371-1

0 9 8 7 6 5 4 3 2 1

Contents

Preface

Educational Use of Poetry

These poems may be experienced for general reading pleasure.

However, for educational purposes, they may be utilized by teachers and other interested individuals—perhaps parents—in providing limited specific instructions in English grammar while preserving the major objective to provide instruction in literature comprehension and analysis.

In literature classes the teacher, or a student involved in self-study, will, at least, deal with literature comprehension and literature analysis. The teacher may utilize discussion groups and/or summary analytical report-writing or individualized self-study assignments in which each student is expected to exhibit a comprehension of the assigned material by means of a written analysis.

In English grammar classes, each haiku poem may be presented by the teacher as an English language example of the simple sentence, the main sentence students must experience, comprehend, and create in written expression before proceeding to the creation and the utilization of the three other English language sentences: namely,

1) The compound sentence
2) The complex sentence
3) The compound-complex sentence

Therefore, haiku poems give students essential examples for accurately expressing themselves in the form of a written simple sentence whatever view or idea that is perceived.

Me: The New American Teenager

I am the new American teenager.
I am a brand-new teenager in the year 1992.

I have a newly designed brain.
My brain consists of new patterns of behavior—patterns of
    behavior that are beneficial to society as well as to
    myself.

My newly designed brain provides me with
    immense self-love,
    a clear-cut self-concept,
    tremendous self-pride,
    self-determination, and
    will power.

Within me is a new, early-age innate tendency to be
    individualistic, unlike various forms of the planet Earth's
    plant and animal groups that seem unable—for good or
    bad reasons—to function as a separate, distinct creative
    entity.
I have no built-in need for crowds, groups, mobs, tribes, or
    gangs.

I am not from Venus, Saturn, Jupiter, or Mars or any of the
    other nearby planets.
I am an Earth human with a newly designed brain.

I now conclude that the human body is a magnificent life
    form.
The human body contains a brain that can accomplish
    wonders.
The human body deserves utmost respect.

I shall respect my body.
I shall give it the best of care.
I shall instill within it a noble character.
I shall represent the most beneficial human values, such as
respect for the law, self-respect, respect for the rights of
others, even if I never join an organized group of
humans.

Henceforth, I shall concentrate on the Self.
I shall utilize it for beneficial accomplishments.
I shall give it the best of care.
I shall keep it fit and never intentionally put into it such
destructive substances as alcoholic beverages or
destructive plant drugs.
I will not do that.
I shall not do that.
I will not destroy my magnificent human body that contains
the kind of a brain no other life form on Earth possesses.

I shall not draw into my Self smoke containing tars from
burning cigarettes.
I do not ever want to regret once having a wonderful human
machine.
I want to always possess a wonderful human machine that
can be of benefit to me and my country.

I want to live a beneficial life utilizing my Self.
If society—all other humans—benefit from my
self-preservation methods, good! I hope so.
If society—all humans—do not benefit from my
self-preservation methods, that is absolutely too bad!

As a teenager, I shall show utmost respect for my Self.
I shall use my magnificent brain and resist being influenced
by repetitive, current disruptive forms of behavior
exhibited by numerous adults in our society. Some
adult humans seem to want the worst of everything for
themselves as well as others.

I do not like faded blue denims, leather jackets, and
chewing gum.
Some so-called adults do.
I like leather sport coats and unfaded denims of any color.

My brain is filled with individualized concepts of
self-reliance, self-respect, and self-appreciation.
To me the Self is supreme.
To me the Self is great.
To me there must be tremendous respect for the Self.

I must be a superior human on Earth at all times.
I must not deface, mar, or despoil any property, public or
private.
I must not commit a crime and disrespect myself.

I attend public school to learn.
I am not going to talk in classroom to any kind of a friend.
I shall listen to the teacher and quietly do my classroom
work.
I plan to be one of the smartest students in the history of the
human race on the planet Earth.
I shall never be superstitious.
I am becoming so scientific that only concrete evidence is
now needed to prove anything to me.

My brain is being trained to function only in a scientific
    manner.
Day after day it is being trained to use the scientific method
    to manage all problems.

If I must lie, cheat, steal, be corrupt or thoroughly immoral
    in order to have a friend, then I shall do without a
    friend.
I do not ever want any friend I cannot do without.
I shall follow my Self.
I shall not be led by drunkards, drug addicts, or other
    disruptive persons.

I am an American.
I have extreme self-respect for the human body.
I am too proud of my body to put anything even minutely
    destructive in it.
I shall not put beer in it.
I shall not put any other forms of alcoholic beverages in
    it—especially whiskey.
I shall not smoke cigarettes or cigars and inhale the smoke
    into my body.
I am proud to be egotistical to the point of appearing
    ridiculous.

I shall be careful in accepting freinds
I want no friend I cannot do without.
I want no friend that is: namely,

a liar
a thief
an alcoholic drunkard

I am against any form of guitar playing that results in
    emotionally stressful screaming, yelling, or
    grammatically incorrect sounds.

Only words from Longfellow, Shakespeare, Emerson,
　　Einstein, Freud, Dickinson, and other such persons shall
　　I allow to influence my young mind.
I am totally against rock-music sounds and hippie talk.
I prefer the use of standard English in every area and on
　　every level of communication in American society.

I have supreme respect for the human body.
The human body is a machine to be extremely admired.
The human body is the most advanced life form on the
　　planet Earth.
Its brain can accomplish wonders—miracles—where the
　　skills of analysis, creativity, and evaluation should be
　　utilized.
Therefore, the human body must never be defiled with any
　　destructive liquid or solid substance that can internally
　　destroy it within any period of time.
Thus, my newly designed, teenaged brain does not accept
　　superstitious imaginings or beliefs.
My teenaged brain was designed to utilize the scientific
　　method only.
My teenaged brain is a brain that was designed to deal in
　　analysis, creativity, and evaluation in the field of
　　science.

But what else do I stand for with my newly designed
　　American, teenaged brain?
I stand for brushing my teeth at least twice a day.
I stand for flossing my teeth after every meal during the day.
I stand for massaging my gums at least once a day.
My teeth and gums are essential parts of me.
Therefore, I think they deserve as much respect and care as
　　any other part of me.

And again, and as a reminder, I am the arrogant, egotistical, American youth with a newly designed brain.

I am the one who is too proud to put deadly plant drugs into my invaluable Self.

I am the one who is too proud to follow the crowd and intake into a magnificent human body alcoholic beverage of any strength.

I am the self-centered American youth who is proud of a glorious, grand Self even if non-other has such a comprehension or realization.

I stand for high values.

My friends will not mean more to me than I do to myself.

Friends mean nothing to me if they are to interfere with my scientific progress.

I stand for high scholastic achievement.

I will cooperate with my teachers and help to provide a quiet learning environment whenever expected.

I shall learn what is taught by the teacher.

I shall not talk or in any other way misbehave in any teacher's classroom.

I shall do homework daily if that is what my teachers expect.

I shall not earn bad grades and become a disruptive force in our society.

I shall respect public and private property

I shall never despoil public or private property with graffiti scribblings.

I consider such behavior as a form of disrespect for the invaluable Self as well as for one's country in spite of its shortcomings.

I am an intellectual.
I am a health-conscious human.
I possess immense self-respect for the human body.
I shall protect the health of my Self.
I shall make beneficial use of my brain.

I Love the City

I love the city

I love the city's asphalt streets and concrete sidewalks.

I love the city's magnificent buildings.
    I love the shiny, black, square-paneled,
    glassy ones that reflect the sunlight
    and every mood of the day.
    I love the tall 50-, 60-, 70-storied
    buildings and those even higher.

I love the city's colleges, universities, and public libraries
    that can be found in every direction throughout the city.

I love its crowds, all of which are busily
    engaged in various activities as
    some sit at desks high up in office
    buildings, some clerk in stores,
    some ride up and down in elevators while
    many are well-educated and quite sophisticated
    men and women.

I love the city's inexpensive lunch stands as well as its
    expensive restaurants.
I love the hot dogs, the hamburgers at the fast-food stands,
    the roast beef and the baked turkey at the cafeterias,
    and the steaks and baked potatoes in the fancy
    restaurants where I may sit, slowly eat, relax, think, and
    drink an awful lot of coffee.

I love the city even with its many problems. I hope it will
    have its problems solved and exist forever.

I Stood beneath a Tree

I quietly stood beneath that tree
   in the city park.
A yellow leaf floated down to the ground
   in front of me.
I felt something on my shoulder.
I looked around.
There was a leaf that had not reached the ground.
A cool breeze blew.
The sky was clear.
The sunlight was warm.
And the sounds of children's voices
   were near.

What Is Haiku Poetry?

Haiku was originated by the Japanese. It is created under a strict seventeen-syllable count. The *haiku* is a three-line, unrhymed poem composed of five syllables in the first line, seven syllables in the second line, and five syllables in the third line.

Most American writers do not always follow the strict seventeen-syllable count. Sometimes they use eighteen syllables, the reasons being the distinct differences between the Japanese and English languages. Nevertheless, all *haiku* creators follow the basic rule that each poem consists of one English-language simple sentence.

The Rosebush

The rosebush produced
red and white roses for
everyone's pleasure.

The Dolphins

The intelligent
dolphins treated the life-jacketed
child with care.

The Human Race

The human race must
improve and stop verging on
total disaster.

The Young Plant

A young green-leaved plant
with a white stem stood in rich,
fertile, Earth soil.

The White Lily

A magnificent
white lily stood alone in
the evening twilight.

The Ocean Waves

White-crested ocean
waves smashed themselves against
weathered rocky cliffs.

The Red Sky

The red sky of the
setting sun backgrounded the
city's skyscrapers.

The Thunderstorm

The thunderstorm sent
torrents of rain water to
the dry desert floor.

The Twilight Sunlight

The twilight sunlight
cast long sand-castle shadows
on the nice beach.

The Venice Canal

The Venice canal
now flowed cleanly through Venice
into the sea.

The River

The river flowed
between snow-covered shores
and quiet farm lands.

The Mountain Stream

The white, foamy mountain
stream rushed down the dark
twisted channel home.

The Architectural Beauty

The architectural
beauty of the city
at night was charming.

The City Hall

The city hall was
starkly white in the blue
early morning twilight.

The City

It was a city
of busy freeways, white mountaintops
and blue skies.

The Big City at Night

The big city was
beautiful at night with its
galaxy of lights.

The Farmhouse

The brown, forlorn,
weather-beaten farmhouse stood in
a brown field of grass.

The Birds

Chickadee birds and
pigeons give Los Angeles an
added grace and charm.

The Clouds

Heavy, puffy, white,
rain-bearing clouds curtained
distant mountainsides.

The Cool Day

The cool, sunny day
was appreciated after
hundred-degree days.

The Babies

After a comfortable
sleep lovely babies
sang a wordless song.

The Rising Sun

The rising sun's beam
of light glistened on the
surface of the lake.

The Precipice

I stood at the precipice
with the ocean and roses
at my feet.

The Ocean Waves

The fierce ocean waves
smashed themselves against the
huge, black, coastline rocks.

The Captive Zoo Audience

The captive zoo au-
dience accepted the cur-
ious visitors.

A Gray Pigeon

A gray pigeon walked
in the morning sunlight
outside my window.

Three Chimpanzees

Three nice, black chimpan-
zees placidly sat togeth-
er on the brown ground.

A California Beach Day

The cool, bright beach morning
began with the roaring sounds of
the Pacific Ocean and voices of thousands
of beach-goers moving toward the sandy
Pacific Ocean shores
from city paths
and automobile parking lots,
seeking choice spots to spend the day
in sunlight
and in cool, strong ocean breezes.

White sea gulls, in bright Southern
California sunlight, flew overhead,
swerving and drifting,
with outspread wings
while down below
white-crested ocean waves roared toward
the Pacific shores of California,
finally spilling themselves all along the
shores in the pleasingly bright sunlight
while beach-goers, children and adults,
played or sat on the beach sands
while the strong, cooling ocean wind
continued to blow toward the beaches.

Bicycle riders rode their bicycles along
a fourteen-mile bicycle path paralleling
the peopled beaches and the turbid
Pacific Ocean.

Surfboard riders skillfully rode
Pacific Ocean waves toward the shores
and returned again and again for
more rides and more spills.

Roller-skaters occupied themselves in
their areas with twirls, skillful jumps,
and other carefully executed forms of
exercise on their roller skates in the
bright sunlight and the cool ocean breeze.

Above all, the California sky was a
cloudless blue while the sun moved
slowly but relentlessly across the sky
and everything below.

So with the passage of time beyond
morning and noon there appeared
a golden sunset cresting the
ocean's surface at the western horizon
and painting the sky a brilliant russet
red as it continued its fiery disappearance
down and beneath the horizon.

The beach-goers reluctantly began to
gather their belongings as well as themselves
who were still engulfed in an environment of
soft, sandy beaches, the sounds and sights
of white, crested ocean waves,
cooler ocean breezes,
and the now-golden rays of a sun
now out of sight beneath the horizon.

The Human Race

The human race is quite a run.
Participation is a requirement.

What a race!

The race is quite a challenge.
It travels through lifetime conditions
involving peace and war,
accomplishments and failures.

The race goes on with the inevitable
passage of seconds, minutes, hours
and days and years and lifetimes.

The human race goes on.
Some runners are winners.
Some runners are losers.
Some runners are good and some are evil.

There are no exceptions
All planet Earth runners are required
to participate fully.
That is the way of life.

Even eliminations did not exist.

Self-Preference

On this planet Earth
one should not
belong to anyone but one's self.

That is enough cooperation with the
human race in one's lifetime.

A lifetime being too brief
for all forms of life,
one should dominate one's self
and proceed
to reach great educational goals
in human development,
in psychology,
in self-mastery,
in science's basic values,
in technology
along with selected, indestructible
personal values
which resist successfully
all potential controls by forces
outside of the self.

An individual may take extreme pride
in intellectual accomplishment
as an individual,
in never having one's brain ursurped by
detrimental forces,
in never having one's teen-aged and adult
individuality dominated by psycho-sociological
forces outside of the self.

Unsavory Togetherness

Sometimes being stagnated,

Sometimes creeping,

Sometimes standing not moving along
    at all with multitudes of other
    humans

Provide evidence

That human togetherness is a detriment

    to individual accomplishment;

    to pure individuality;

    to pure self-domination;

    and to pure development of an
    indestructible self-concept.